T0052522

The Split History of

WORLD WAR I

ALLIES PERSPECTIVE

BY MICHAEL BURGAN

CONTENT CONSULTANT:
Timothy Solie
Adjunct Professor
Department of History
Minnesota State University, Mankato

COMPASS POINT BOOKS
a capstone imprint

Compass Point Books are published by Capstone,
1710 Roe Crest Drive, North Mankato, Minnesota 56003
www.capstonepub.com

Library of Congress Cataloging-in-Publication Data
Burgan, Michael.
 The split history of World War I: a perspectives flip book / by Michael Burgan.
   pages cm.—(Perspectives flip books)
 Includes bibliographical references and index.
 Summary: "Describes the opposing viewpoints of the Allies and the Central Powers during
World War I"—Provided by publisher.
 ISBN 978-0-7565-4694-6 (library binding)
 ISBN 978-0-7565-4700-4 (paperback)
 ISBN 978-0-7565-4702-8 (ebook PDF)
 ISBN 978-0-7565-4704-2 (reflowable epub)
 1. World War, 1914–1918—Juvenile literature. I. Title. II. Title: Split history of World War One.
   D522.7.B87 2014
   940.3—dc23   2013007019

MANAGING EDITOR
CATHERINE NEITGE

LIBRARY CONSULTANT
KATHLEEN BAXTER

DESIGNERS
GENE BENTDAHL AND SARAH BENNETT

PRODUCTION SPECIALIST
LAURA MANTHE

MEDIA RESEARCHER
WANDA WINCH

IMAGE CREDITS

Allies Perspective: "The American soldiers in the presence of gas, 42nd Div., Essey, France."
Sept. 20, 1918. (Reeve #037283) OHA 80: Reeve Photograph Collection. Otis Historical Archives,
National Museum of Health & Medicine, cover (top); Capstone, 13; CRIAimages.com: Jay Robert
Nash Collection, 6, 14, 28; Library of Congress: Prints and Photographs Division, cover (bottom),
10, 17, 19, 21, 23; National Archives and Records Administration, 25, 26; Wikimedia: Bibliothèque
nationale de France/Le Petit Journal, 5

Central Powers Perspective: "The American soldiers in the presence of gas, 42nd Div., Essey,
France." Sept. 20, 1918. (Reeve #037283) OHA 80: Reeve Photograph Collection. Otis Historical
Archives, National Museum of Health & Medicine, cover (bottom); CRIAImages.com: Jay Robert
Nash Collection, 12, 15, 17, 18, 24, 29; Getty Images Inc: adoc-photos, 27, Keystone, 11, Historical,
26, Hulton-Deutsch Collection, 23, Time Life Pictures/Mansell, 5; Library of Congress: Prints and
Photographs Division, cover (top), 8, 20

Art elements: Shutterstock: Color Symphony, paper texture, Ebtikar, flag, Sandra Cunningham,
grunge photo, SvetlanaR, grunge lines

Table of Contents

THE GREAT WAR BEGINS

In his office in London, Sir Edward Grey opened the first of several telegrams that would soon shock the world. It was June 28, 1914. Grey was the foreign secretary of Great Britain. He read the news that Archduke Franz Ferdinand, who was next in line to rule the Austro-Hungarian Empire, had been shot and killed in Sarajevo, the capital of Bosnia and Herzegovina. Grey knew that the assassination could lead to a huge conflict—for Britain and the rest of the world.

The killer, Gavrilo Princip, was a Bosnian Serb with close ties to the military of Serbia. He supported Serbia's desire that Bosnia and Herzegovina become independent from Austria-Hungary.

A 1914 Paris newspaper illustration depicts Gavrilo Princip firing the fatal shots.

Russia's leader, Tsar Nicholas II, supported Serbia in its aim to weaken Austria-Hungary in that part of Europe, known as the Balkans.

Britain had long tried to remain independent from the other major European powers. It focused more on building an overseas empire. But since the 1870s, nations with shared interests had formed alliances. Austria-Hungary, Italy, and Germany created one of these alliances. France and Russia, worried about the growing economic and military strength of Germany, formed another. Great Britain joined France and Russia in 1907 to create the Triple Entente.

For weeks after the assassination, Grey and other leaders in Europe waited to see if Austria-Hungary would respond with a military strike. They worried such an attack could spark a much larger war.

Austria-Hungary sent a list of 12 demands to the Serbian government on July 23. The Serbs accepted all but two— demands that would virtually end their independence and give Austria-Hungary control over their affairs. The Serbs then reached out to Russia, which promised to help them fight a war. Germany had already promised Austria-Hungary it would enter the war if Russia did.

Three days later Grey tried to organize a conference of European ambassadors to stop the threat of a large-scale war. The idea went nowhere. Grey told a German official that if war began, "it will be the greatest catastrophe that the world has ever seen."

Austria-Hungary fired on Serbia on July 29. They were the first shots of what would come to be called the Great War. Soon the fighting spread north, as German troops moved through Belgium and Luxembourg on their way to France.

Belgium and Luxembourg were neutral, although both had good relations with Britain and France. The British had promised to help defend Belgium if Germany attacked. On August 4 Great Britain declared war on Germany, and eight days later it declared war on Austria-Hungary. Joining the British were its dominions of Canada,

Belgian soldiers march to war in 1914.

ANGER IN THE BALKANS

In October 1908 Austria-Hungary upset people around the world by annexing the small Balkan province of Bosnia and Herzegovina. The move sparked anger and protest from many Bosnians. People in the neighboring nation of Serbia were also outraged. Serbians dreamed of a united Slavic nation that included Serbia, Bosnia and Herzegovina, and other nations in the Balkans.

Australia, New Zealand, and South Africa and its colonies. The British said they were fighting to protect independence and other values that were "vital to the civilized world." Britain also wanted to keep Germany's power under control.

Germany and Austria-Hungary would later get help from Bulgaria and the Ottoman Empire, which was based in what is now Turkey. Germany was the main military power of this group, called the Central Powers.

In the Triple Entente, Russia and France had the largest armies, while Britain had a powerful navy. Soon after declaring war, Britain sent a small land force to help France fight the Germans. Several million more troops would follow in the months and years to come. But in the first weeks of the war, the French and Belgians did most of the fighting against Germany.

For the French, the war was about defending itself from a German attack. But France also wanted to regain Alsace-Lorraine, a region to its northeast it had lost to Germany after an earlier war.

France counted heavily on Russia's help. Together with Great Britain, France and Russia were now known as the Allies.

THE TWO FRONTS

France attacked the Germans in Alsace-Lorraine, but most of the heavy fighting took place farther north in France and Belgium. The British Army's first major action took place at Mons, Belgium, in August. Despite being outnumbered more than two to one, the British fought so well that the German commander thought they were using machine guns instead of rifles. But the larger German forces gained the upper hand and forced the British to retreat. German troops then continued their advance on Paris, the capital of France. By September French casualties were more than 260,000. Along the Marne River, the Allies stopped the invading enemy, who began to retreat September 9. Several thousand French reinforcements had piled into 600 taxicabs in Paris to reach the battle.

In October some of the heaviest fighting took place near the Belgian city of Ypres. The Germans managed to take some land, but the Allies remained in the region. They were determined to keep all the territory they held, even though they were paying a high cost in casualties.

Russia's army was the world's largest with 1.4 million troops, but it had trouble against the Central Powers. The Russians had had some success in Galicia, which was part of Austria-Hungary. But they had then suffered a major defeat against the Germans at the Battle of Tannenberg at the end of August. Over the next several months, the Russians continued to fight with no major victories. As 1914 ended the Allies realized they faced a long war against a determined enemy.

YEARS OF DESTRUCTION

roops moved freely across the battlefield in the

war's early months. But by 1915 the war centered on trenches

on the Western Front, a line stretching more than 450 miles

(725 kilometers) across northern France between the Swiss border

and the North Sea. The men lived in the trenches and used them for

protection from enemy attacks. The land between Allied trenches

and the enemy's was known as no man's land. British trenches

were about 7 feet (2 meters) deep and 6 feet (1.8 m) wide, although

the sizes varied. As fighting moved from one area to another, the

soldiers built more connecting trenches, creating complicated mazes.

An abandoned British trench, which was captured by the Germans

British soldier Arthur Maitland wrote his parents that he stayed in the trenches almost all the time. The Germans "shell us constantly but we laugh at them from our burrows like rabbits." But a fellow soldier, Neville Woodroffe, wrote home about the huge number of deaths he saw and said, "This is a terrible war." He was killed a month later.

Even as the Allies tried to kill the Germans, the two sides did at times realize their enemies were human. In December 1914 British and German soldiers in parts of France and Belgium shared what was called the Christmas truce. They stopped fighting for the holiday. They sang Christmas carols, and German soldiers set up Christmas trees. Enemy troops even came out of the trenches to shake hands with each other. But after Christmas was over, the soldiers once again returned to the war, determined to beat their enemies.

BATTLES BEYOND EUROPE

The Great War soon spread beyond land. With its powerful navy, the British formed a blockade against Germany. The British stopped ships that were delivering supplies to its enemy. They seized any materials they thought might help the Germans, including food and cloth.

Many European nations had colonies in Africa and Asia, and fierce fighting went on in those places as well. In the Pacific Ocean, troops from Australia and New Zealand seized German-controlled islands. Japan had joined the Allied cause in August 1914. British soldiers helped Japanese troops take Tsingtao, a city in China that Germany controlled. In Africa battles took place in what is now Tanzania and Namibia. Both the British and French also used residents of their colonies to fight in Europe. Although not called a world war at the time, the Great War was truly worldwide.

Some of the major fighting in Asia took place on the western edge of the continent. When the Ottoman Empire, based in present-day Turkey, joined the Central Powers, British military leaders wanted to take the battle to the Turks. British troops eventually fought across the Middle East, which was then mostly part of the Ottoman Empire. Allied troops planned to invade the region at the Gallipoli Peninsula on the European side of the Dardanelles, a narrow strait that divides Europe and Asia. The Allies knew if they controlled the Dardanelles, they could push forward to the Ottoman capital, Constantinople (now called Istanbul).

The first of about 70,000 Allied forces came ashore at the Gallipoli Peninsula starting April 25, 1915. Many of the troops were from Australia and New Zealand. In the months to come, those forces faced heavy losses as they tried to push out the Ottoman troops. A major offensive failed in August. One New Zealander, Charlie Clark, later described hearing "thump, thump, thump and it was fellows falling around me. Nine or ten of them, suddenly wounded or dead ..." The Allies pulled out their troops early in 1916. The Dardanelles invasion was a daring military move that ended badly. But it did keep Turkish troops from fighting the Russians.

FIGHTING BACK IN EUROPE

The Dardanelles campaign lasted almost a year. During that time fighting continued on the Western Front, though neither side made major gains. The two sides had clashed near Ypres, Belgium, in April 1915. This time French troops faced a new danger—chlorine, a gas that is poisonous in large amounts. German soldiers opened steel tanks to release the gas, which drifted over French troops in their trenches. One French soldier described his reaction to the gas attack: "It burned my throat, caused pains in my chest and made breathing all but impossible. I spat blood and suffered dizziness. We all thought that we were lost."

The Allies fought back by developing gas masks to protect their soldiers and shells that could fire gas at the Germans. But gas warfare did not always work as planned. At the Battle of Loos in autumn 1915, British troops watched in horror as gas aimed at

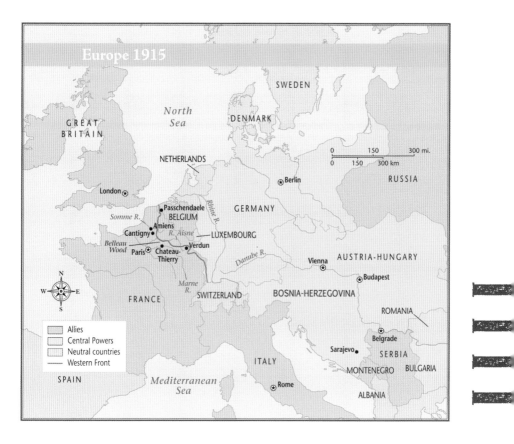

the Germans drifted back toward them. The gas injured more than 2,600 British soldiers and seven died.

On the Eastern Front, which covered Russia, Germany, and Austria-Hungary, Russia continued to suffer against its enemies in 1915. The Allies also saw Serbia finally fall to the Central Powers, after it had resisted several invasions. During 1915 the fighting also spread to Italy, which had joined the Allies. In a secret deal, the Allies offered to give some Austrian territory to Italy if it helped fight the Central Powers. But Italian soldiers struggled when battling Austro-Hungarian troops near the Alps between Austria and Italy.

MAJOR BATTLES OF 1916

As 1916 began the French could see German activity near the city of Verdun, France. Several forts surrounded the city. After losing Fort Duoaumont at the end of February, the French could have pulled back. Instead General Philippe Pétain was determined to fight for Verdun. His artillery fired on the German troops, and French fighter planes took to the skies. They shot down German planes and fired rockets at German balloons. A road leading into Verdun saw a constant stream of French trucks bringing food, supplies, and more soldiers to the city.

French troops take cover during the Battle of Verdun.

NEW WAY OF FIGHTING

In 1915 the British began working on a new weapon, the tank. The British designed a war vehicle with armor to protect troops inside, a gun, and metal treads that would let it roll over trenches. The first British tank, the Mark I, entered battle in September 1916. By the end of the war, the Allies had built several thousand tanks. The most commonly used model, the FT 17, came from France. The Germans had trouble building tanks that performed as well as the Allied tanks. German soldiers sometimes used captured Allied tanks instead.

Through the rest of the year, the two sides battled for control of Verdun. The French took back land the Germans had won earlier. When the fighting finally ended, the Germans saw how hard it was to push out well-supplied French forces fighting in their own country. They would not launch another major offensive until 1918. But the French paid a high price, with about 400,000 casualties.

To draw away German troops from France, Russia launched a daring new offensive in the east. General Alexei Brusilov commanded the attack. Starting in June his troops rolled through the Austro-Hungarian forces, who were surprised by the attack. They thought the system of trenches they had dug, some up to 20 feet (6 m) deep, would keep the Russians away. Instead, as Russian troops quickly moved forward, the Austrians became trapped in the trenches. The Russians captured about 400,000 prisoners before Central Powers' reinforcements slowed their advance. The Brusilov Offensive showed the Russians at their best on the battlefield. But it also cost them almost 500,000 casualties.

The third major campaign of 1916 came in the west, along France's Somme River. This time the British led the way, under the command of General Douglas Haig. The Battle of the Somme turned into a bloody, ugly struggle. The British were counting on their artillery to clear out front-line German troops in late June. Then British soldiers would move forward to fight the remaining soldiers. But the British didn't have enough guns and shells to destroy German artillery. Meanwhile, the Germans had time to set up their machine guns and fire on the British soldiers. In just the first day, July 1, the British suffered nearly 60,000 casualties, including nearly 20,000 dead. Soldiers carried off the wounded using whatever they could find, including wheelbarrows and wooden planks. After that brutal day, both sides launched small offensives, without major gains.

In September British tanks rolled through battlefields for the first time. Many broke down or were destroyed, but they did help the British make some gains. Heavy rainfall in October turned the battlefield into a sea of mud and hampered progress by either army. The German Army retreated in November, but it wasn't a victory for the Allies, who had suffered more than 600,000 casualties. About two-thirds of those were British.

THE HOME FRONT

At the start of the war, Great Britain relied on volunteers for its military. But by 1916 it was drafting young men to join the army. The other Allies were already using a draft. Some people in Britain were pacifists, meaning they opposed all war. The government did

French women work in the fields without horses. Retreating German soldiers took the animals with them.

allow men to avoid fighting if they had religious or moral reasons for opposing the war. But some of the men who refused to fight were tried and sent to prison.

In all the Allied nations, civilians faced food shortages, and food was often rationed. People could buy only limited amounts of sugar, meat, and dairy products. In England the government took control of the railroads and raised taxes for the war effort. Cities and towns used parkland to raise crops.

Women played a large role on the home front. They went to work in factories to build weapons or plow fields once farmed by men. Some British women learned how to defend themselves and their families as part of the Women's Defence Relief Corps. The women were also trained to replace men in factories so the men could join the military. Women also got close to battle, serving as nurses. Some did more than help the wounded. Edith Cavell was a British nurse living in Belgium when the war broke out. She helped Allied troops escape Belgium. The Germans arrested and killed her for her actions. Another British woman, Flora Sandes, went to Serbia when the war began and fought for that country.

CHANGING FORCES

hile the war waged in Europe, Americans closely followed the action. Millions of immigrants had come from countries now battling each other. Tens of thousands had already returned to Europe to help defend their homelands. U.S. businesses shipped goods to the Allies. The United States was technically neutral, but President Woodrow Wilson and many Americans favored close ties with Great Britain. The two countries had strong business relations as well as a shared language.

A 1915 British army recruitment poster

An incident in May 1915 increased American anger with Germany. The British passenger ship *Lusitania* was sailing from New York to England. Along with almost 2,000 people, the ship carried war supplies for the British. On May 7 a German submarine fired a torpedo at the ship off the coast of Ireland. American citizen Michael Byrne later described hearing "a thunderous roar, as if the skies opened" when the torpedo exploded. As the lifeboats near him quickly filled, Byrne jumped into the water and began swimming until another lifeboat rescued him. Byrne was lucky. The German attack sank the *Lusitania* and killed nearly 1,200 people, including 128 Americans.

Across Great Britain and the United States, people criticized the deadly German attack. Former U.S. president Theodore Roosevelt called it a "vaster scale of murder than old-time pirates ever practiced." U.S. President Woodrow Wilson demanded that Germany admit that the killing of neutral American passengers was illegal. Germany refused. In September 1915, though, it did agree to attack only armed merchant ships or warships.

WILSON REACHES A LIMIT

Wilson tried to get the Allies and Central Powers to discuss peace at the beginning of 1916. That effort failed, but the Germans did agree to stop attacking armed merchant ships without warning. As the war dragged on, though, Germany changed its mind. In January 1917 it once again vowed to attack any ships off British waters without warning. Wilson cut off diplomatic relations with Germany on February 3.

Wilson's anti-German feelings increased in late February after he learned about an earlier German offer to Mexico. The British intercepted a coded telegram sent in January by a German official to the German ambassador to Mexico. The telegram said that in case the U.S. joined the Allies, "we make Mexico a proposal of alliance on the following basis: make war together, make peace together, generous financial support and an understanding on our part that Mexico is to reconquer the lost territory in Texas, New Mexico, and Arizona."

Wilson asked Congress to declare war on April 2, saying, "The world must be made safe for democracy." Congress voted to do so four days later. U.S. troops began preparing for war.

At first the United States' decision didn't change much on the battlefield. The Allies launched the Nivelle Offensive in April 1917 in central France, which they hoped would end the war within two days with few casualties. But French casualties alone were about 40,000 in just one day, and the army gained almost no land. Some French soldiers, tired of war and so many losses, refused to fight. General Pétain, who replaced Nivelle, increased soldiers' leave to help morale.

British soldiers drag a small cannon through the mud.

In July another battle began outside Ypres, with the British leading the attack. General Haig fought on even as rain created huge fields of mud. His men showed signs of losing their fighting spirit. One British soldier later wrote, "If you got hit, the chances were you slipped into some yawning shell-hole full of greyly opaque water concealing unmentionable things and you drowned there." The British did manage to gain a small bit of land in the three-month battle, but at the cost of more than 300,000 casualties.

In the east Russia had gone through a revolution. Tsar Nicholas II was imprisoned and a new government now controlled the military. The Russians launched a new offensive in July, but the Germans soon counterattacked and scored several victories.

By fall the new Russian government was under assault from its own people. Russian socialists called Bolsheviks, who wanted government ownership of farms and factories, came to power. Led by Vladimir Lenin, the Bolsheviks asked the Germans for peace. The Allies lost one of their major militaries and were angry that the Russians had abandoned them. Allied leaders also feared that the

Bolsheviks would try to spread socialism in Europe. With Russia out of the war, the Germans were free to move many troops from the Eastern Front to the west.

HEADING TO EUROPE

The first U.S. forces reached France in June 1917, under the command of General John "Black Jack" Pershing. They were met by cheering crowds who believed the Americans would help the Allies win the war.

Germany had now increased its submarine war, and ships crossing the Atlantic with U.S. troops and supplies were favored targets. To fight back the Allies used convoys—large groups of ships defended by naval vessels. By July 1917 several dozen U.S. warships were based in Europe, helping with the convoys.

As in other Allied countries, war changed daily life for many Americans. The U.S. government created propaganda to stir up hatred for the Central Powers, especially Germany. Support for the war was not particularly strong. Many Americans had ties to Germany, and most Irish Americans disliked the British, since they had treated the Irish badly in their homeland. Some Americans were pacifists or socialists who opposed the war.

The propaganda against Germany sometimes made life hard for German-Americans. In some places local governments no longer allowed schools to teach the German language, and musicians refused to play German music. A few German-Americans were beaten or even killed for alleged disloyalty to the United States.

As in Europe, the U.S. government took control of parts of the economy to help the war effort. The War Industries Board directed companies to make supplies for the military. The Food Administration encouraged Americans to grow more of their own food so farmers' crops could go to the troops. The National War Labor Board kept good relations between companies and workers, so the workers would not strike. Large strikes were a problem for the French and British.

American gardeners were urged to back the war effort.

The war led to other changes in the United States. As in Europe, women began to work in factories. Large numbers of African-Americans moved off southern farms to work in northern cities. They were part of a "Great Migration" that saw about 500,000 blacks leave the South during the war. And while the war stopped most immigration to the United States from Europe, nearly 900,000 Mexicans entered the country between 1910 and 1920.

Through 1917 Americans at home mobilized for war as U.S. troops trained in Europe and took part in several battles. The next year they would finally fight in large numbers on the battlefields of France.

PEACE AT LAST

*T*he Allies faced heavy losses, particularly on the Western

Front, through 1917. The Central Powers, though, were losing their

will to fight. German leaders no longer expected to win the war,

but they wanted to launch several last major offensives and grab as

much land as possible.

The first offensive came in March 1918 along the Somme. The

British were forced to give back land they had won at the battle

there in 1916. Large German guns began to shell Paris. But starting

in May, American troops began to play a role in stopping the

German advance. They won a battle at Cantigny, and in June

American soldiers on the front line in France

helped the Allies win the Battle of Belleau Wood. Though they lacked training, the Americans fought hard, leading Australian officer Edwin Trundle to write, "I'm sure the Yanks are going to prove excellent fighting troops."

A FINAL PUSH

The Allies began several major counterattacks in July, starting along the Marne River and then in Amiens. By the end of August, American General Pershing was planning to use his forces against the Germans near the town of St. Mihiel. But Marshal Ferdinand Foch of France, who was in charge of the other Allied forces, had different ideas. He wanted to move some of the Americans to other locations. The two commanders began to argue, with Foch asking if Pershing wanted to go to battle. "Most assuredly," Pershing replied, "but as an American army."

Foch finally agreed to keep the Americans together. They fought at St. Mihiel. In late September they moved north to the Argonne Forest. There and along the Meuse River, the Americans faced their

An American gun crew attacks the German position.

toughest fighting of the war. More than 26,000 soldiers were killed
and 95,000 wounded in the fighting, which lasted into November.

James "Slim" Jones fought in that campaign. He later recalled
how he and just six other men attacked a German machine gun
position "with all pistols blazing ... we got 132 prisoners and
captured nine machine guns."

The Allied successes during the fall convinced British and French
military leaders that the war would soon be over. But the Germans
refused to give up. As the Germans pulled back to a defensive
position known as the Hindenburg Line, British artillery rained shells
on them. By late September the Allies had broken through the line. At
almost the same time, Bulgaria agreed to stop fighting in the Balkans.
It was the first of the Central Powers to seek peace.

Meanwhile, the British were gaining ground against the Ottoman
Empire in the Middle East. In the Alps between Italy and Austria,
the Italians now greatly outnumbered their weakened enemy.
October fighting along the Piave River led to an Italian victory.
German leaders were finally ready to discuss ending the war.

THE 14 POINTS

In January 1918 President Wilson had proposed 14 Points that he thought should shape the peace process. Wilson wanted to end the Great War in a way that would lead to lasting peace and spread democracy across Europe. His points included the return of French land from Germany, including Alsace-Lorraine; independence for the various ethnic groups in Austria-Hungary and the Ottoman Empire; a free Poland; and an international organization that would protect each nation's independence and work to prevent future wars. As for Germany, Wilson said, "We do not wish to injure her or to block in any way her legitimate influence or power."

The fighting stopped November 11, 1918—at the 11th hour of the 11th day of the 11th month. People celebrated the armistice across Europe. A U.S. soldier in Paris, George Alexander, described the scene: "Paris went wild in about two minutes. People flocked out into the streets—until it was almost impossible to drive thru ... Well—we shipped our baggage on ... and went crazy with the rest of Paris. Never before in my life was I hugged—kissed—and pushed about—as much."

Germany agreed to give up most of its military equipment and release prisoners of war. Meanwhile, the Allied blockade continued as the two sides discussed peace. The Allies, though, didn't allow Germany to attend the peace conference that began in Paris in January 1919. The Allies would decide the terms of peace—and Germany would have to accept them.

The peace conference showed strong differences among the Allies. Wilson was determined to keep his 14 Points at the center of

The leaders who shaped the Versailles Treaty (from left, seated): Vittorio Orlando of Italy, David Lloyd George of Great Britain, Georges Clemenceau of France, and Woodrow Wilson of the United States.

the discussion. But British Prime Minister David Lloyd George and French Premier Georges Clemenceau wanted to punish Germany as much as possible. While Wilson had called for creating several new independent states, the other Allies had already signed secret treaties that divided up lands in the Ottoman Empire and former German colonies. But a number of independent countries did emerge in Europe, including Finland, Poland, Czechoslovakia, and Yugoslavia.

The Allies also argued over reparations. Britain and France wanted Germany to pay a high price. To Wilson, excessive reparations would give Germany "powerful reasons for wishing one day to take revenge." But Wilson was willing to go along with reparations and other British and French demands, as long as the peace treaty created the new international organization he sought. The Treaty of Versailles did call for a League of Nations.

The final peace treaty forced Germany to give up land, greatly reduce the size of its military, and take blame for starting the Great War. Many of the new countries formed in Europe came out of the Austro-Hungarian Empire. Italy also gained land from the Austrians, and France took control of western Germany.

Not everyone was happy with the final agreement. Marshal Ferdinand Foch of France said the treaty the Allies and Germans signed was not peace, it was "an armistice for 20 years." Foch thought another huge war was bound to erupt in Europe. And he was right.

Some U.S. lawmakers disliked the treaty, especially the part about the League of Nations. They didn't want the United States dragged into future European wars. The country hadn't suffered as much as France or Great Britain. Still, in just six months of major combat, about 50,000 Americans had been killed in battle. More than that died of disease. A worldwide flu epidemic that spread among the troops killed both soldiers and citizens. And like the soldiers of other countries, thousands of Americans had come home "shell-shocked." Their mental health suffered because of the horrible things they had experienced in Europe. Today this condition is called post-traumatic stress disorder.

In the end, dozens of nations joined the League of Nations. But the United States was not one of them. The league could not prevent another European war—a war started in 1939 by Germany. World War I had left Germany weak, and many Germans wanted to rebuild their military and once again show their strength. World War II had many causes—one of them was the harsh peace the Allies called for after World War I.

INDEX